GERM FREE ADOLESCENT

by Natalie Mitchell

Epsilon Productions & The Bunker Theatre present
GERM FREE ADOLESCENT
29th October – 9th November 2019

GERM FREE ADOLESCENT
by Natalie Mitchell

CAST

ASHLEY	Francesca Henry
OLLIE	Jake Richards

CREATIVE TEAM

Director	Grace Gummer
Designer	Lizzy Leech
Lighting Designer	Sherry Coenen
Sound Designer	Nicola Chang
Projection Designer	Heather Pasfield
Production Manager	Zara Janmohamed
Stage Manager	Millie Jones
Casting	Monica Siyanga
PR	Jemma Last PR
Community Engagement Facilitator	Ellie Fulcher
Producer	Epsilon Productions

GERM FREE ADOLESCENT was originally commissioned and developed by Script Club, with seed funding from Greenhouse (the House Network) in partnership with LV21, the Brook Theatre, Mid Kent College and Medway CAMHS.

Thank you to Sam Wainwright for rehearsal and production shots.

CAST AND CREATIVE TEAM

FRANCESCA HENRY | ASHLEY

Theatre credits include: OUR TOWN (Regent's Park Theatre); DEAR ELIZABETH and SONYA R&D (Gate Theatre); THE WOLVES (Theatre Royal Stratford East); STORMZY X ADIDAS ORIGINALS – IMMERSIVE THEATRE EVENT (Adidas & Jukebox Collective); WATER WINGS R&D (Old Vic).

Productions whilst training include INTIMATE APPAREL (Richard Burton Company) and SPILT (Richard Burton Company/Royal Court).

Film and TV credits include: DOCTORS (BBC) and forthcoming feature film 2.0 LUCY (Shopfloor Films).

Francesca trained at The Royal Welsh College of Music and Drama.

JAKE RICHARDS | OLLIE

Jake recently graduated from ArtsEd in West London. He was born and raised in Maidstone, Kent, before moving to London to study a BA (Hons) Degree in Acting at ArtsEd where he was nominated for a Laurence Olivier Bursary Award and awarded the Leverhulme Arts Scholarship to help fund his acting training. He made his professional stage debut recently in THIS WOUNDED ISLAND by Natalie Mitchell (Theatre503).

NATALIE MITCHELL | WRITER

Natalie Mitchell writes for television, theatre and radio. She is currently writing a ten-part podcast drama for BBC Sounds alongside co-writer Vickie Donoghue; is under commission to Synergy Theatre Company; was the only writer named on the Edinburgh TV Festival's Ones To Watch 2019 scheme and was named on the BBC Talent Hot List 2017.

Theatre work includes CAN'T STAND ME NOW as part of the Royal Court Young Writers' Festival; CRAWLING IN THE DARK (Almeida Theatre); WHEN THEY GO LOW (National Theatre Connections) and GERM FREE ADOLESCENT and THIS WOUNDED ISLAND, both of which were created with and for non-traditional theatre audiences in Kent. She has also had plays presented at the Soho, Hampstead and Finborough Theatres. TV includes episodes of HOLBY CITY, DOCTORS, ACKLEY BRIDGE and two years as a core writer on EASTENDERS. Radio includes PROUD for BBC Radio 3 and THE MAN WHO SOLD THE WORLD and HIDDEN HARM for BBC Radio 4.

GRACE GUMMER | DIRECTOR

Directing includes: ROMAN CANDLE by Tom Fowler (Theatre503/Edinburgh Festival Fringe); SOUTHALL PARK by Amarjit Basan (Watford Palace Theatre); REALITY by Stuart Slade (Royal Court/RWCMD/Gate Theatre); SENSE, THEATRE FROM THE WINDOWS (Open Court Festival, Royal Court); H, TYPICAL, THE HIGHER WE GO, THE SYSTEM (The Big Idea, The Site, Royal Court); BUTTER (VAULT Festival; Origins New Work Award); ANONYMOUS ANONYMOUS (The Space).

Grace was Literary Associate at the Royal Court in 2019, and Trainee Director 2016–17.

Associate and assistant director credits include: BAD ROADS, Associate (Royal Court); RE:HOME and DRAWING PLAY, Associate (The Yard); GLASS. KILL. BLUEBEARD. IMP., GUNDOG, VICTORY CONDITION, ROAD, ANATOMY OF A SUICIDE (Royal Court); BEYOND CARING (The Yard/National Theatre Shed); LINES, QUDZ (The Yard).

LIZZY LEECH | DESIGNER

Lizzy trained at Bristol Old Vic Theatre School and studied English Literature at Warwick University.

Recent designs include: TO MY YOUNGER SELF (Synergy Theatre); A TABLE TENNIS PLAY (Walrus Theatre/Theatre Royal Plymouth); THE MERCHANT OF VENICE (Stafford Festival Shakespeare); CYMBELINE (Royal Central School of Speech and Drama); THE BUTTERFLY LION (The Barn Theatre, Cirencester); HANSEL AND GRETEL, FAIRYTALE DETECTIVES (Theatr Clwyd); SONGLINES (HighTide Theatre); THE LEFTOVERS (Leicester Curve); A GIRL IN SCHOOL UNIFORM (WALKS INTO A BAR) (New Diorama Theatre/Leeds Playhouse); ALBY THE PENGUIN SAVES CHRISTMAS (Oxford Playhouse); NOYE'S FLUDDE (Blackheath Halls Children's Opera); DON GIOVANNI (Waterperry Opera Festival); VANITY FAIR (Middle Temple Hall); LOVE FOR LOVE and THE HERESY OF LOVE (Bristol Old Vic).

Forthcoming designs include: SPIDERFLY (Theatre503); JOAN OF LEEDS (Breach Theatre/New Diorama Theatre); ANTIGONE (Holy What!/New Diorama Theatre).

As Assistant Designer: PERICLES (National Theatre); BEGINNING (National Theatre/West End); MACBETH (Royal Shakespeare Company); A TALE OF TWO CITIES and OLIVER TWIST (Regent's Park Open Air Theatre). lizzyleech.com

SHERRY COENEN | LIGHTING DESIGNER

Sherry has been lighting shows in the US and UK since graduating with a BFA in Lighting Design from the University of Miami.

Shows include: OPERATION MINCEMEAT (NDT) *KOI nominated 2019*, FRANKENSTEIN (BAC) *KOI winner 2019*, THE SINGING MERMAID (Little Angel Theatre); IZINDAVA (UK tour); THIS IS HOW WE DIE (UK tour); CINDERELLA (Queen's Theatre Hornchurch); SKIN TIGHT (Park90); CELL (UK tour); CONQUEST OF THE SOUTH POLE, THESE TREES ARE MADE OF BLOOD (Arcola Theatre); BRRR! (UK tour); 5 GUYS CHILLIN' (King's Head Theatre); ANTON CHEKHOV (Hampstead Theatre).

NICOLA CHANG | SOUND DESIGNER

Nicola is a composer/sound designer for theatre, film and commercial media across the UK, US and Asia. As a performer, she currently plays for SIX (West End) as Dep Keys/Musical Director and she is a former cast member of STOMP! (West End/world tour). She is also an Artistic Associate of the King's Head Theatre and a BFI x BAFTA Crew Member.

She has performed at the Royal Albert Hall, the Royal Festival Hall and the Shakespeare's Globe as a percussionist, and holds a MMus in Composition from King's College London. Additionally, she is a Composer and Musical Director attached to British Youth Music Theatre UK.

Her theatre credits include: THE ICE CREAM BOYS (Jermyn Street Theatre); LITTLE BABY JESUS, THE TEMPEST (Orange Tree Theatre); WILD GOOSE DREAMS (Theatre Royal Bath); THE KING OF HELL'S PALACE (Hampstead Theatre); THE DEATH OF OPHELIA (Sam Wanamaker Playhouse, Shakespeare's Globe); SUMMER ROLLS (Park Theatre); WHITE PEARL (Royal Court); FROM SHORE TO SHORE (Royal Exchange Theatre, Manchester/UK tour); LORD OF THE FLIES (Greenwich Theatre); DANGEROUS GIANT ANIMALS (Tristan Bates Theatre); FINISHING THE PICTURE (Finborough Theatre); A HUNDRED WORDS FOR SNOW (Arcola Theatre) and THE FREE9 (National Theatre).

HEATHER PASFIELD | PROJECTION DESIGNER

Heather is a Digital Producer for Media and Performance. Her work includes filmmaking, live streaming and projection design to explore digital methods of storytelling and improve online access to theatre.

STAGING SISTERHOOD (Southbank Centre and Seenaryo; Digital Producer); BABYLON: BEYOND BORDERS (Bush Theatre; Live Stream Producer); ARES (VAULT Festival; Video Designer); THE DIVIDE, SYLVIA, WOMEN OF THE OLD VIC, MARCH FOR WOMEN (Old Vic; Young Digital Creator 2018); TEDx The Next Stage 2017 (The Embassy; Live Stream Producer); EDINBURGH FRINGE FESTIVAL 2016/7 (The Pleasance; Media Futures Photographer) A Studio Season (Complicité; Digital Marketing Assistant).

Training: The Royal Central School of Speech and Drama, The University of Exeter.

ZARA JANMOHAMED | PRODUCTION MANAGER

Recent work has included: WE ANCHOR IN HOPE, FUCK YOU PAY ME, BOX CLEVER/KILLYMUCK and GROTTY (Bunker Theatre); EDINBURGH FRINGE (Mick Perrin Worldwide); Shakespeare UK and European tour, RADA Festival); DRAMATIC DINING CABARET and ROTTERDAM (RADA); THE AMBER TRAP (Theatre503); HOARD, SITTING and MRS DALLOWAY (Arcola Theatre).

Stage Management: DICK WHITTINGTON AND HIS CAT, 80th ANNIVERSARY GALA (Oxford Playhouse); A PASSAGE TO INDIA (Park Theatre/tour); RAISING MARTHA, KILL ME NOW (Park Theatre) and SCAPEGOAT (St Stevens Church).

MILLIE JONES | STAGE MANAGER

Millie has worked for theatres and companies such as Kneehigh, Little Angel Theatre, WildWorks, C-Scape Dance Company, o-region and Hall for Cornwall, in many and varied roles including Stage Manager, Tour Manager, Production Assistant and Art Department Assistant. Alongside this she has produced independent projects, and has managed to work in the 'normal' world too, for places such as the *Guardian* and business development consultants Just Add Water.

ELLIE FULCHER | COMMUNITY ENGAGEMENT FACILITATOR

Ellie is a facilitator who works with young people and community groups to make and write theatre. Ellie has worked with a number of theatres and community spaces across London such as, The Yard Theatre, National Citizens Service, Harrow Arts Centre. Ellie is the participation facilitator at the Royal Court Theatre.

EPSILON PRODUCTIONS | PRODUCER

An award-winning production company that for the past 13 years have produced theatre that has strived to bring difficult subject matters to the stage. We aim to make theatre that fires debate and brings people together but, most of all, to tell good stories well.

Notable productions include NOT TALKING by Mike Bartlett (Arcola Theatre); STATE VS JOHN HAYES by Lucy Roslyn (Argus Angel WINNER for Artistic Excellence UK and NYC); CHICKEN SHOP by Anna Jordan (WINNER Best London Fringe Production, Park Theatre); CRYSTAL SPRINGS by Kathy Rucker, SKIN TIGHT by Gary Henderson (Park Theatre).
www.epsilonproductions.co.uk

With four concrete pillars marking out a large thrust performance space, an eclectic mix of audience seating on three sides of the stage, and a craft beer bar, The Bunker is a visceral and unique performance space with a character of its own.

The Bunker believes in artists. We give ambitious artists a home in which to share their work with adventurous audiences. We are champions of each piece that we programme and we want to ensure our stage is filled with exciting, exhilarating, and contemporary theatre featuring artists that represent the world that we live in.

The Bunker was opened in October 2016 by founding directors Joshua McTaggart and Joel Fisher. The theatre's first year of work included the award-winning sell-out show SKIN A CAT and Cardboard Citizen's 25th Anniversary epic HOME TRUTHS. In-house productions have included festivals MY WHITE BEST FRIEND (AND OTHER LETTERS LEFT UNSAID) and THIS IS BLACK as well as DEVIL WITH THE BLUE DRESS and the double bill KILLYMUCK & BOX CLEVER.

In September 2018, Artistic Director Chris Sonnex joined Executive Director David Ralf to lead the theatre's dedicated team, several of whom were involved in the original conversion of the space. Bunker Theatre Productions CIC is a not-for-profit theatre, which currently receives no public subsidy.

Find Out More
www.bunkertheatre.com
Box Office: 0207 234 0486
E-Mail: info@bunkertheatre.com
Address: 53a Southwark Street, London, SE1 1RU

The Bunker Team

GERM FREE ADOLESCENT

Natalie Mitchell

Acknowledgements

This play wouldn't exist without Jane Fallowfield, who has supported, pushed and believed in me for a long time. Thank you to everyone who contributed to the development process: Lauren Heritage and CAMHS; Roy Smith and Medway Youth Services; Robyn Goldsmith and Debs Pinder at Medway Council; Paivi at LV21; Richard Kingdom at Greenhouse and every single young person who came to a workshop or watched the show. Thanks also to Sam Swann, Sandra Reid, Alex Austin, Amy Bowden, Daisy Young, Liz Bacon and Ros Terry. Thanks to Sam Wainwright, Nick Barron and Nicole Schivardi. Thanks to the whole creative and production team at The Bunker who achieve miracles under challenging circumstances – particularly David and Chris who don't just give it the biggun but actually act – taking a massive punt on me and my little play. And finally thanks to Grace Gummer for never letting me off the hook.

N.M.

Germ Free Adolescent originally toured Medway, Kent, in October 2015 with the following creative team:

ASHLEY	Amy Bowden
OLLIE	Alex Austin
Director	Jane Fallowfield
Designer	Daisy Young
Producer	Elizabeth Bacon

Characters

ASHLEY
OLLIE

This text went to press before the end of rehearsals and so may differ slightly from the play as performed.

1.

ASHLEY   Tracey has thrush. At least, I'm pretty sure she
has. She wants me to have a look but she knows
I won't so I don't know why she asks.

T is for Thrush.

Vaginal thrush is a yeast infection that is usually
caused by a type of fungus that lives naturally in
the vagina.

Typical symptoms include itching and soreness,
pain during sex (Trace reckons it killed when she
shagged Chris Chambers, and he's not that big
apparently) and cottage-cheese discharge.

So it seems like a textbook case. Thrush.

She's not happy when I tell her she can't have sex
till it clears up. It's not an STI, but you can still…

You can still pass it on if you…

You can pass it on.

Do I need to…

Maybe I should…

No. No.

I write down the name of the medication she needs
(Caneston Combi is the one everyone on the
forum recommends) and take three quid off her.

Trace is always reluctant to pay, cos this surgery
was kind of her idea, but she gets a ten-per-cent
cut of the takings so she's only cheating herself by
not paying.

Why am I giving out sexual-health advice?

Well. A few months ago Trace had chlamydia and I diagnosed it.

See, I'd read –

I'd read a lot about it.

C is for Chlamydia.

THE most common sexually transmitted infection in the UK. Passed on from one person to another through unprotected sex.

In 2018, two hundred and eighteen thousand, and ninety-five people tested positive for chlamydia in England. Sixty per cent of those were under twenty-five years old.

Older people shouldn't be smug though, because the largest proportional increase in diagnoses came in the over-sixty-five age group.

Yeah.

It's easily treatable with antibiotics. That's what I told her.

Tracey.

Because it is.

And she was appreciative.

Then she suggested I could make a bit of money giving this kind of advice out. As I know so much.

About…

About…

And I know people can go to the 'sexual-health hub' at Clover Street but –

You know.

Can be a bit awkward.

So I run my clinic three lunchtimes a week. People can come and ask me anything.

I lay out my leaflets, four on each subject and let people look through them. They're not allowed to take them away though.

There needs to be four of each.

After she pays (reluctantly), Tracey asks me if I'm ready for tonight.

The big night.

Nudge nudge, wink wink.

The night that me and Ollie are going to…

Me and Ollie are going to…

OLLIE   When me and Ashley first started going out I got a message off Mike Reeds. Well it was anonymous but I knew it was Mike, cos he's the only twat who'd send something like that.

It said 'Your girlfriend's dog rough.'

My dad reckons I should've knocked him out.
I wanted to.

But –

I didn't.

I know some people think Ash is a bit… funny.

A bit –

But I think she's gorgeous.

Always have.

To be honest.

Didn't have the guts to tell her though.

Not for ages.

The thing is right, she's never been in a group, if you know what I mean.

She weren't in school enough. She was hardly in at all in Year 10. People said it was cos she was pregnant, but Tracey used to go and see her all the time and she said that was bollocks.

Even though everyone knew that her and Connor Beecham had...

You know.

Which actually really pissed me off, because she knew I didn't like Connor. Not since Year 7 when he took the mick out of my leg, pretending to walk like a... You know.

So I took my leg brace off and smacked him round the head with it.

Got suspended for a week for that.

So I like, I did kind of take it personally. That she would... With him.

Cos we were sposed to be friends. Known each other since nursery. We didn't speak much during school but –

Sometimes happens don't it? Didn't mean we weren't friends.

She used to sit in the library and that, with people like Paul.

And I used to spend all my time playing football with the lads. Mike, Rob, Chris and that.

Yeah.

Even with my leg.

I never used to mind when they called me spaz, cos I knew it was just...

It was pure bants, you know. Chris has a stutter and we'd take the mick out of him for that too so...

It was funny. You know.

We were mates.

Then we started sixth form and, you know.

I just…

I wanted to…

I saw Ash walking home one day and just couldn't hold it in any more.

I shouted after her –

'Ashley!'

'I fancy you!'

And that was it.

…Amazing.

Even though Mike called Ashley a dog.

ASHLEY   I know Tracey is looking at me waiting for a reply but I can't speak.

My tummy's gone all funny and tight and I'm trying to do that soothing rhythm-breathing thing that Annie taught me, counting the breaths in my head.

I'd been trying to pretend it wasn't going to happen.

Tonight.

It's our three-month anniversary.

Me and Ollie.

Three months.

He's got the house to himself so we're going to…

We're supposed to…

When he asked me my heart was pounding and my brain was like a computer, scrolling through the thousands of reasons why I shouldn't, why I couldn't…

C is for Chlamydia.

G is for Gonorrhoea

T is for Thrush.

But this is what I've been working up to.

This is what I want.

To be normal.

OLLIE   Three months is officially my longest relationship.
Previous record held with Becky Forrester, six
weeks and two days.

She dumped me for Mike.

But whatever.

My mum and dad are out tonight, watching some
ska tribute band in Gillingham, so me and Ash
will have the place to ourselves.

And the thing is –

We haven't… Yet. S'not like I haven't wanted to,
but I didn't want to rush things. You know. Cos
the thing is –

With Becky it was… It was…

Well.

I don't like to think about it to be honest.

It's not like you can ask anyone about it either,
is it?

I tried to watch stuff online but –

I'm not sure –

I mean.

Maybe it's been Photoshopped.

Can you Photoshop porn?

My dad gave me a condom ages ago but –

He never told me much. Too embarrassed, I think.

And it's not like I can go to Ash for advice can I, like everyone else does. I know she's more experienced than me. She must be mustn't she, to know all the stuff she does?

I think she thinks I'm... I think she thinks, that cos I've been out with a few people that I am too. But I'm – not. Not really.

Obviously I have. Obviously, Fat Tracey in Year 10. Everyone has with Tracey. Everyone.

Becky Forrester, like I said.

And then Rachel Wilde in Year 11 but that was a bit... Well.

I kind of don't like thinking about that either because, well, actually – it might not count.

No, I'm counting it.

I don't know if she does. I never asked.

Maybe I should.

Should I?

No. I'm just going to count it.

Sounds better anyway.

Three. Soon to be four.

Hopefully.

If she – wants to.

With me.

And it will be special. If we do.

Because.

Because it's Ash.

It needs to be perfect.

2.

ASHLEY   I spend all afternoon trying to work out how I can avoid going to Ollie's. I even consider asking Tracey to do that thing where you press on someone's neck really hard until they pass out.

Cos if I pass out at school, I won't have to...

No.

My last lesson of the day is double history. European political history. Nazis and stuff.

Trace is giggling to herself, cos she read somewhere that Hitler was in to watersports. She nudges me.

'Who knows, maybe Ollie'll be in to that too.'

I ignore her.

We're reading about Kristallnacht when a kid from the year below knocks on the door. He's got a bunch of roses in his hands.

For me.

From Ollie.

...

Everyone's staring but I just focus on spelling out Kristallnacht over and over again so there's no space for any other thoughts.

There's no way I can cancel on him tonight after this.

OLLIE   The roses are the first part of my surprise for Ash.

A couple of years ago Rob McLennan from two years above, did it for his girlfriend on Valentine's Day. Loads of people said he was a total prick for doing it, but the girls thought it was amazing, which is all that matters really isn't it?

I really hope she likes them. I don't know what her favourite flowers are but –

Should I have found out?

I should have found out shouldn't I?

Argh! What an idiot!

If she doesn't mention them, I won't either. I could even pretend they weren't from me.

ASHLEY   I've got a couple of hours to kill after school so arrange to meet Polo Paul by the statue opposite Wickes.

It doesn't have a cone on its head today.

Probably will once the Tap 'n' Tin kicks out.

We sit here a lot, me and Paul. He doesn't know about... No one knows about it.

Obviously.

Paul's got his own stuff going on.

About six months ago he came to see me in the clinic. He was being kind of cagey about what he wanted.

It was only after he left that I realised I only had three of my Stonewall leaflets left, instead of four.

And I always have four.

Four of each leaflet.

I never mentioned it to him. Didn't want to put him on the spot.

Replaced the leaflet and carried on as normal.

But I'm pretty sure he knows that I know, if you know what I mean.

We meet at the statue, and I've got my notebook with me.

We've been keeping a list of the prostitutes who work round the back of Wickes, categorising them by age and appearance.

Youngblack.

Oldred.

Shortblondeteeth

It's a bit like a David Attenborough study.

We sit eating Cadbury's Creme Eggs and I want to tell him about tonight. About Ollie.

About…

But how can I without…

It's getting harder to hide all these thoughts.

So I tell him a half-truth.

That I'm scared.

He hugs me (which is fine) and says that it's pretty normal to feel like that on your first time.

It's normal to feel like this.

It's normal to be scared.

So maybe the way my mind keeps tricking me isn't so mad after all.

Maybe it's normal.

I'm normal.

OLLIE   The second part of the surprise is that I'm cooking for her.

Chicken Kiev and chips. My dad wasn't sure it was a good idea, because of all the garlic, but it's her favourite, so who cares about a bit of garlic?

Once Mum and Dad have gone out, I take a long shower.

Not massively long, probably just about nudging the five-minute mark (environment and that) but I want to make sure I haven't missed anything.

I usually use the Radox but my mum's got this special stuff that Dad got her for Christmas –

I think it's by Gok Wan or someone like that, so I decide that as this is a special occasion, I'll give it a go.

Ash has never mentioned my smell before.

Not that I smell bad or anything.

I don't think I do.

She's never mentioned it.

Maybe that means she doesn't like it?

Or does her not mentioning it mean that she does like it?

I take my jeans off and on again.

My favourite ones are still in the wash, which is really annoying. I had a proper go at Mum about that. They're my favourite because they fit nicely but not so tight that you can tell my leg is...

These ones are alright. If you know what you're looking for, you can tell my legs aren't even, but I don't think Ash will be focusing on that.

I mean, I hope she isn't.

When I was with Becky, she used to...

Sometimes she'd say...

She'd take the mick. You know.

About my leg.

Just bants and that.

I wonder if I could do it without taking my jeans off?

Then she wouldn't see my leg at all.

But then I'd have to leave my socks on and that's not exactly... sexy.

Is it.

Or we could just keep the lights off?

Yeah. That's what we'll do. Keep the lights off.

I've put the condom my dad gave me in my bedside table.

I wish he'd given me more than one cos I... I'm... you know, sometimes when you put it on things go wrong and...

I've used them before.

Obviously.

I just don't want anything to go wrong.

Not this time.

Not with Ash.

ASHLEY   When I get to Ollie's I want to turn and run. But I don't.

I stand for a moment, still. The CD in my head telling me all the things that will...

All the things that *could* happen tonight.

That could happen. That could happen but...

That could happen but it will be alright.

I will be alright.

OLLIE   Ash looks fit!

She seems a bit –

Distant. Like her mind is somewhere else. But she looks great.

She doesn't mention the flowers so I don't either.

I shouldn't have sent them should I?

She doesn't eat much.

I hope it's not cos I overcooked it. Or maybe garlic was a mistake. I try to remember where my chewing gum is.

ASHLEY   I feel sick.

I wonder for a minute whether it could be the food. Almost seventy per cent of supermarket chickens are infected with Campylobacter.

But I suppose that doesn't include Kievs.

It doesn't include Kievs.

It can't include Kievs.

No.

Ollie's okay so…

It's not the food is it.

It's me.

It's tonight.

It's this.

…

I go to the toilet and sit on the floor. Last time I was here the lock didn't work but it does now.

I count my breaths.

It could happen but it will be alright.

It could happen but it will be alright.

I start to spell out the word KRISTALLNACHT in my head.

After ten times I feel calmer.

OLLIE   I tidy up while Ash is in the loo, and go and find the chewy.

I sit on the sofa waiting for her to come out.

I don't want it to look like I'm waiting, but I don't want to put the telly on in case we end up watching it all night.

So I just sit.

I forgot to tell her how pretty she looks.

Cos she does.

I hope she's not annoyed with me.

ASHLEY   Ollie is sitting really awkwardly on the sofa.

It's like, he's trying really hard to seem relaxed, but looks really stiff instead.

Maybe he's as nervous as I am? Maybe I should just tell him…

I can't.

I can't because…

Because…

No.

He wouldn't get it.

No one gets it.

Because it's mental.

I look at his little moon face and long legs tucked awkwardly under him and think how amazing he is, and how amazing it is that I've managed to keep this secret from him for so long.

And I suddenly feel…

Exhausted.

I go and sit next to him and he folds his arms around me in the way that makes me feel safe, and begins to kiss me.

As long as he's got his arms around me like this, it's okay.

It's safe. Like this.

It took ages for me to feel comfortable with the kissing but…

It's safe now.

It could happen, but it'll be alright.

He tastes of garlic and mint.

OLLIE   How do you move things on in a natural way?

Should I ask her if she wants to go upstairs? Or do I just take her hand and lead her up there in a manly way?

And what about my socks?

ASHLEY   We're kissing and it's alright. It's more than alright.

I can't wait to tell Annie at our next session that I did this.

And it was ALRIGHT.

She'll be really proud of me.

It's even alright when he puts his hand under my top and undoes my bra.

Every time I feel myself tense up I...

K-R-I-S-T-A-L-L-N-A-C-H-T.

Yes.

It could happen but it will be alright.

OLLIE   I take my shirt off and think about taking my jeans off but don't.

Not yet.

I feel her stomach muscles tense under my fingers. She must be ticklish.

I try again.

She tenses again.

ASHLEY   K-R-I-S-T-A-L-L-N-A-C-H-T.

OLLIE   She grabs my hand. Holds it.

Stops it.

...

She –

Doesn't want to, does she?

She doesn't want to.

With me.

ASHLEY   I really want to.

I want to so much.

OLLIE   She won't look at me.

ASHLEY   I can't look at him cos I think I might cry and
I don't know how he'll take that.

OLLIE   Am I really that bad?

ASHLEY   I sit up and do my bra back up.

His face is all concerned and worried.

Because of me.

Because

I'm a freak.

OLLIE   We sit.

Silent.

ASHLEY   I could explain.

Maybe he…

Maybe he *would* get it?

OLLIE   The silence stretches on, suffocating.

What is so wrong with her?

I've done everything right, you know. I've bought
her flowers, cooked.

I've, I've been respectful.

But she –

I can feel myself getting –

Properly wound up.

ASHLEY   If I could…

If I could just…

If I could just say it.

…

I turn to him.

He's got this twisted, ugly look on his face that
I've never seen and before I get a chance to speak,
he spits –

OLLIE   'What the fuck is wrong with you?'

She looks at me, her eyes all shiny.

Not a word.

I want to grab her, shake her.

Tell her how shit she's made me feel.

'Prick-tease.'

She stares at me.

Her face crumples and she –

She walks out.

3.

ASHLEY   K-R-I-S-T-A-L-N

No that's not right.

K-R-I-S-T-A-L-N

Fuck!

K-R-I-S-T-A-L-L-N-A-C-H-T

K-R-I-S-T-A-L-L-N-A-C-H-T

It feels good at first.

Then it's not enough.

I check to see…

There's no one around.

…

I see a parked car, and touch its wing mirror.

If I touch the wing mirrors of all the parked cars I pass, then me and Ollie will work it out.

We'll work it out.

We'll work it out.

I know I shouldn't be doing this.

I know.

But it feels like…

For that moment.

Everything's okay.

And the relief is…

The release is…

It's amazing.

But then I need to do it again.

And again.

And again.

I slow down as I get near mine cos I don't want Mum and Dad to know.

They think I've told Ollie everything.

As if.

I haven't told anyone everything.

Not Ollie, not them, not Tracey and Paul.

Not even Annie.

How do you explain something that only makes sense in your head?

How do you make people understand that everything you do, every day, is controlled by thoughts that you know are irrational, but no matter how hard you try you can't make go away.

And it feels so good…

You don't want it to go away.

I'm trapped and I can't get out.

When they first noticed things were…

When they first noticed…

When they noticed.

Mum was suffocating.

'You alright love?'

'You okay?'

'How you feeling?'

But that was better than –

Dad.

He told me to get a grip.

Get a grip.

I sneak in the front door and head up to my room.

If I'm quiet enough they won't realise I'm home, and I'll have enough time to…

Mum won't let me have a lock on the door.

It's been hard for her.

Seeing me like this.

So I push my swivel chair up against the door.

I switch the main light off and bring my lamp down to the floor beside the bed.

Ollie's angry twisted face.

I pull out the shoebox marked A to D. Then E to G, and so on, lining them up as I go.

Taking each box in turn, I count the leaflets. Four of each.

I close my eyes and pick one leaflet out of each box at random.

C is for Chlamydia

G is for Gonorrhoea

T is for Thrush.

Ollie's twisted face.

C is for Chlamydia

G is for Gonorrhoea

T is for Thrush.

Do I need to…

Maybe I should…

No. No.

I didn't.

We didn't.

It's okay because we didn't…

We didn't.

OLLIE   I think I might cry. But I don't.

Not cried since my hamster died.

Teen Wolf.

Even then I think it was more because of my hayfever.

I've got that weird in-between feeling where you're angry and upset at the same time and don't know what to do.

I thought Ashley was better than that.

Better than Rachel Wilde and the...

Better than Becky Forrester and her snide remarks about...

Better than all of them.

But she's not.

She's the same.

They're all the same.

I can't believe I was taken in.

I feel like such a...

I run upstairs to my room looking around for something, anything that will stop me feeling so...

So argh!

I punch the wardrobe.

I considered the wall but I was worried it might be a bit hard so went for the wardrobe instead but actually, plywood is a lot harder than you think it'll be.

Really hard, actually.

It hurts.

I leave a small dent in it, and a much bigger one in my knuckle, which starts to bleed.

I pick at the loose skin which stings and makes it bleed more, but in a weird way makes me feel better.

What happened plays over and over again in my head. I can't work out how it ended up so...

Ashley's shiny eyes.

Scared.

Of me?

Maybe I should message her.

But what would I say?

Sorry?

No.

I bought her flowers, cooked her dinner.

I was nothing but respectful.

No.

I'm not the one who did anything wrong.

My knuckle's still bleeding.

I put it in my mouth to see if that stops it.

Her face, scared.

...

I know I shouldn't've called her a prick-tease but –

No.

No!

She should be apologising to me!

Making me look like an idiot.

Making me think she actually liked me.

I bite down on my knuckle.

Hard. It makes my eyes water.

She's messed *everything* up.

And I want her to hurt as much as I do.

ASHLEY   I put the leaflets back in their boxes in reverse order and slide them back under the bed.

My heart's no longer racing and I can breathe normally again.

No one would know I'd…

I'm fine.

Nothing happened so I'm fine.

…

But we did…

He did…

Do I need to…

Maybe I should…

Maybe I should have a test, just to be on the safe side.

I'll go online, see what everyone in the forum thinks.

See if I need to…

…

My Insta is open.

And I see…

I see…

Ollie.

He's taken me out of his bio.

4.

OLLIE   I spend the weekend at home.

I feel awful.

Sick.

My belly aches, my throat's tight and my eyes are burning.

When I tell Dad I'm too ill to go Millwall with him, I'm not even lying.

I feel awful.

Really awful.

He reckons it's a waste of my season ticket.

We have a bit of a row about it.

Mum's got the hump too, about me missing Sunday lunch at Auntie Linda's. She's one of those aunts who's not a real aunt, d'you know what I mean?

They went to school together or something.

And actually I would like to go cos she does a proper good roast but...

I stay in bed.

Have some toast.

We've run out of butter cos Mum doesn't do the food shop till midweek.

It's dry. Like swallowing razor blades.

Gets stuck in my throat.

I really do feel awful.

ASHLEY   The last thing I wanna do is go to school on Monday, but I've worked so hard to...

To seem normal.

I can't let this...

I won't let this give me away.

OLLIE   I'm dreading school on Monday.

Cos everyone'll know.

They'll all be looking at me.

Laughing.

…

That I can't even…

…

So I bunk.

ASHLEY   I go in.

Mask in place.

Tracey jumps on me.

'I'm surprised you're in today babe. Thought you might be too upset.'

I bat her away.

'Just didn't work out.'

I think she believes me.

OLLIE   Don't mean to.

Get up, dressed. Walk in like I always do, maybe a bit slower than usual. Bag dragging behind me.

But when I get to the front gate I just…

I'm sure those girls are talking about me.

Laughing.

You know how girls do.

Mike's there.

Casually leaning on his SEAT Ibiza.

Passed his test a couple of months ago, and don't we all know about it.

'Alright?'

'Alright.'

'Going McDonald's. Wanna come?'

We've both got double English first thing, but I'd rather have a Double Sausage & Egg McMuffin any day.

Even if it is with Mike.

We jump in his car and head to the drive-thru on Beechings Way.

Not really spent any time together since I stopped playing football with him and the lads.

After the message he sent about Ashley.

Ashley.

I swallow the sick feeling down.

Mike reckons the lads on the team are really missing me and my left foot.

'Specially since I bulked up.

I'd forgotten how funny Mike can be.

I mean…

He's a prick.

But a funny prick.

I should've listened to him, you know.

And never gone out with that ugly bitch in the first place.

ASHLEY   I've not seen him all day.

He didn't show up for double English.

I thought about messaging him but…

Just kept my head down.

OLLIE   I feel much better after spending the morning with Mike.

Much more like…

Me.

Not whipped any more.

I decide to come back to school for the afternoon.

I've got business studies which I actually really
enjoy.

But also cos Mike made me realise…

I'm better than her, you know.

I mean –

Ashley who?

ASHLEY   I spot him in the canteen and my stomach drops.
Like it does when you're on a roller-coaster.

I think I might be sick.

He's with Traccy.

OLLIE   I'm heading over to join Mike and Rob and that at
a table, when Tracey pulls me aside.

Says she'll speak to Ashley for me if I buy her
a sausage roll.

She's not a bad girl, Trace.

Bit of a slag, cos everyone's had a go on her but…

So what?

She's the only one who never took the mick out
of…

You know.

And she could've.

But she didn't.

And I kind of…

I dunno.

Maybe –

Maybe it would be good to smooth things over
with Ashley.

Not cos I want her back or anything.

Obviously.

Cos I don't.

But…

Just make things easier.

ASHLEY   He's got his arms round her.

OLLIE   I pull her into me for a hug.

It's nice.

For a split second I think about, you know.

Cos that would really wind Ash up.

Not that I care, obviously.

But Tracey pushes me away.

'Don't even think about it dickhead.'

The way she says it, really makes me laugh.

Proper belly laugh.

It's nice.

ASHLEY   He's got his arms round her and they're…

Laughing!

How can he be laughing?

How can he ever laugh again after…

And she's supposed to be my friend!

OLLIE   It's nice.

I feel good.

Then I turn and spot Ash.

ASHLEY   I feel my face crumple and am about to cry when an arm links through mine.

It's Paul.

OLLIE   Arm in arm with Paul.

ASHLEY   'Let's get out of this shithole.'

OLLIE   Arm in arm with Paul.

Thinks he's so cool.

Paul.

Wouldn't spend time with any of us lot.

Was always hanging round with that Turkish kid from the year above.

I feel my face getting hot.

She can't get away with this.

Making a mug out of me again!

That's…

That's out of order.

That is *totally* out of order!

I run down to the classroom where she holds her surgery.

As I pass through the science corridor I slam the door behind me and it smashes.

Fuck!

I don't stop though.

It's not just my face that's hot now.

It's my whole body.

I'm shaking.

I need to, I need to tell her.

Tell her what a bitch she is.

But they're not there.

And there's only one other place they could be.

5.

ASHLEY   Paul takes me to the statue. Someone's managed
           to put one of those big foam fingers on the
           pointing arm.

           I don't know how they get up there.

           We sit in silence for a bit.

           I read the inscription on the statue to avoid
           talking.

           Thomas F. Waghorn.

           Paul offers me a Polo.

           It worries me how many of them he eats – there's
           a warning on the packet, really small, that says
           they may have a laxative effect if you eat too
           many.

           I'm sure he's aware of the potential pitfalls by
           now.

           Paul doesn't push me, just sits there quietly, letting
           me speak in my own time.

           I imagine what would happen if I told him the
           truth.

           If I finally had the weight of this secret lifted
           off me.

           But.

           I can't.

           So I tell him a half-truth.

           That my nerves got the better of me.

           He looks sideways at me.

           Says he knows how it feels to keep a secret, but
           that admitting things might be the best way to deal
           with them.

           Gives me that sideways look again.

I'm a bit confused to be honest. I don't know if he's talking about himself.

Or – about me.

He continues. Tells me about his first kiss.

With a boy.

Oh.

He *is* talking about himself.

It was the Turkish kid from the year above who didn't stay on in sixth form.

'They never tell you about this stuff do they? The stuff people think falls outside of being "normal".'

'But we're all normal aren't we. Just in different ways.'

And suddenly I get it.

He's talking about both of us.

And if he trusts me not to judge him, I can trust him not to judge me.

I'm going to tell him.

The truth.

Not a half-one this time.

OLLIE   I knew they'd be on that bloody bench.

When I see them sitting there, heads together, I just...

I feel like...

It's a wave.

Anger.

I can literally feel it *in* me.

I run over, grab Paul and start punching him.

I can't stop myself.

It's different from the wardrobe. Kind of harder,
but softer too, depending on where I get him.

I'm shouting.

I don't know what I'm saying but I just can't stop.

I can't stop.

I've never been in a fight before.

Not properly anyway.

I used to imagine smashing Mike's teeth right
down his throat until he choked on them.

But I never actually did it.

Course I didn't.

I don't know if this can be classed as a fight
because I'm the only one throwing punches.

Paul is just curled up on the floor, arms around
his head.

Taking it.

Just taking every blow.

Ash drags me off, then goes back to Paul, wiping
the blood off his face.

Blood.

I begin to feel a bit…

Funny.

I wonder whether I should…

I think I've got a tissue in my…

But I look up and see them together and that
feeling just rushes through me again and I shout as
loud as I can.

'Slag!'

I go to hit Paul again but Ash stops me.

ASHLEY   'Paul's gay you idiot.'

As soon as I say it I wish I hadn't. Paul looks from me to Ollie.

Scared, angry.

Betrayed.

He looks at me again, then away.

He walks off, with as much dignity as he can with a bleeding mouth and ripped shirt.

OLLIE   I feel sick as I watch Paul stumble away.

That's not…

I'm not…

My knuckle's split open again.

I look at Ash and bite down on it.

She can't even look at me.

So I…

I…

I run.

ASHLEY   He told me for me, not him.

And I've betrayed him.

I should go after him but…

I can't move.

I've got Paul's blood on my hand and it's…

It's…

Do I need to…

Maybe I need to…

Do I need to get tested?

K-R-I-S-T –

K-R-I-S-T-A-L-L –

Cars have stopped at the traffic lights.

People are looking.

At me.

Paul's blood.

K-R-I-S-T-A-L-L

K-R-I-S-T-A-L-L-N-A-C-H-T

K-R-I-S-T-A-L-L-N-A-C-H-T

It's on me.

K-R-I-S-T-A-L-L-N-A-C-H-T

Blood.

K-R-I-S-T-A-L-L-N-A-C-H-T

Blood.

On. Me.

K-R-I-S-T-A-L-L-N-A-C-H-T

K-R-I-S-T-A-L-L-N-A-C-H-T

It's not working.

It's not working!

K-R-I-S-T

6.

OLLIE   I can't hide the scrapes and bruises from my mum.
But there's no way I can tell her what happened.

So instead I just put my head in her lap and cry.

She strokes my hair, like she used to when I was
little. And things don't feel half as bad any more.

I take the next couple of days off school.

Because if it's nothing to do with Paul, then it's all
to do with me.

And the fact that Ash just doesn't find me...

Just doesn't want to...

I'm disgusting.

When Mum's upstairs doing the ironing, I sneak
down to Dad's shed.

I remember he bought some...

We both went through a bit of a gym phase.

I put ankle weights on the one leg.

You can't see them under my jeans. I've found
some good videos on YouTube too, with exercises
you can do for...

They promise you'll see a change in four weeks.

Then no one will be able to take the piss any more.

No one.

I keep thinking about Paul.

His bloody face.

His bloody face.

The police are probably on their way.

They'll say it was because I... because I'm
prejudiced.

You know.

Against gays.

But I'm not.

I really don't care about that.

But how do I explain how I…

How it happened?

I'm not even sure I know myself.

I think I know where Paul lives so on Thursday when Mum pops into town I sneak out.

Post a little bit of paper through Paul's letterbox.

It says *sorry* on it.

I hope he knows I mean it.

ASHLEY   Mum and Dad won't let me stay off school.

Trying to make sure I keep to a normal schedule.

As if anything will ever be normal again.

One of Mum's friends saw me.

At the statue.

Drove me home.

They wanted to take my leaflets away but I screamed and cried so they let me keep them.

They've got me an emergency appointment to see Annie on Friday.

I actually thought I'd made progress.

Letting Ollie…

You know.

But instead, I've made things a hundred times worse.

Because Ollie's not in school and Paul won't talk to me. I have no one.

Except Tracey.

She's not so bad, Tracey. Been sitting with me every lunch.

She's helping me reorganise my misc folder when Paul comes in.

There's no bruising or anything on his face.
If I hadn't seen it, I wouldn't even know that...

Trace gives me a little sideways look.

A look I've seen before.

Paul gets out a piece of paper and hands it to me.

'Was this from you?'

It has one word on it.

Sorry.

Ashamed, I shake my head.

'It's from Ollie.'

I'd recognise his cursive handwriting anywhere.

'I am though. Sorry. I wish I'd said it earlier.'

Paul nods. Shoots a look at Tracey.

'S'okay. I know you've had other things on your mind.'

What does he mean by that?

'A lot of other things.'

He smiles and gives another sideways look to Tracey.

That sideways look.

Tracey and Paul.

They know.

All this time I thought I was so good at hiding what was going on.

Hiding behind the clinic.

But…

They know.

They know. And they don't hate me for it.

Tracey gives me a hug.

I let her.

Paul watches on.

Probably still a bit –

Angry with me.

I don't blame him.

As Tracey holds me, I cry.

I feel like the prison I built around myself is collapsing.

And it's not as scary as I thought it'd be.

I don't have to…

I don't have to pretend any more.

I root through my misc leaflets folder.

Find the one I want and head off.

No more secrets. No more lying.

OLLIE   I can't even be bothered to play on the PlayStation. That's how crap I feel. I just sit watching *Loose Women*. Thought it might give me some kind of insight into the female mind but if that's what they're all like, I've got no chance.

Why does everything have to be so difficult?

The letterbox goes.

Is it the police?

Is this it?

I get down really low so if they're looking through the front window they can't see me, but as I crawl on my belly towards the door (imagining I'm on special ops) I realise there's no one there.

Just something lying on the mat.

Junk mail probably.

I pick it up.

A leaflet.

I turn it over and over in my hand.

Could be from Ash.

But...

No message.

Nothing.

Just the leaflet.

It's got to be from Ash.

Hasn't it?

7.

ASHLEY   There's a knock at the door.

OLLIE   Alright.

ASHLEY   Alright.

OLLIE   What...

Was this... Did you put this through my door?

ASHLEY   ...Yeah.

OLLIE   Why?

Beat.

ASHLEY   Why do you think?

OLLIE   I dunno.

Beat.

Do you...

Do you have this?

ASHLEY *looks at* OLLIE. *Long silence. It's still hard for her to name it. To own it. She nods.*

You've got this?

Beat.

ASHLEY   Yeah.

Yes. I do.

I have...

I have

OCD.

Obsessive Compulsive Disorder.

Beat.

OLLIE   I didn't really...

I had to google it.

ASHLEY   And?

OLLIE   You really have this?

ASHLEY   Yes.

OLLIE   But I never... I never saw you do anything, you know.

             Like, like...

ASHLEY   Washing my hands, putting things straight, switching things on and off.

OLLIE   Well.

             Yeah.

ASHLEY   That's not what it is.

OLLIE   No?

ASHLEY   No.

             Beat. ASHLEY *can't bring herself to offer any more up.*

OLLIE   So, like... what do you do then?

ASHLEY   I can't explain.

OLLIE   I want you to.

ASHLEY   I can't.

             It's...

             It sounds mental. When I say it out loud.

             And you won't understand.

OLLIE   Try me.

             ASHLEY *stares at* OLLIE *for a moment before taking him to her bedroom. She shows him her leaflets. All of them.*

             Your leaflet collection.

             OLLIE *looks at them. The sheer amount is a genuine surprise. He picks one up about pregnancy.*

ASHLEY   So, like, when I was in Year 10 I was in hospital and stuff.

OLLIE   You weren't pregnant were you?

ASHLEY   No! I got glandular fever.

OLLIE   After kissing Connor Beecham?

ASHLEY   Maybe.

           OLLIE *pulls a face*.

           And…

           When I was in hospital I started collecting these.

           I kind of thought…

           I thought that if I had all this information, and read it out to myself, it would stop me. Stop me getting ill again.

OLLIE   Right.

ASHLEY   But once I started, I couldn't stop. And most of the leaflets were about, you know, sex and stuff. So I started to get these, these thoughts like, if I…

           If I did…

           Stuff.

           You know.

           I'd get ill.

           I'd get all these things.

OLLIE   But you kissed me.

ASHLEY   Yeah I know. It's not…

           As long as we…

           There were things. That you did. And that I did. That kept me…

           Safe.

           Look I told you it doesn't make sense.

OLLIE   No I kind of…

            I kind of get it.

ASHLEY   You don't have to pretend.

OLLIE   I'm not.

            Beat.

            So is this…

            Is this why you…

            Why you wouldn't have sex with me?

ASHLEY   …Yeah.

            OLLIE *can't help but smile.*

            Don't laugh at me. / I knew you'd think it was
            weird.

OLLIE   / No. No I'm not…

            I'm not laughing at you.

            I'm just…

            I'm relieved.

            Cos like, I thought like. I dunno.

            You didn't want to…

            I mean, like.

            You wanted to.

            But not with me.

            Cos of my leg and that /

ASHLEY   / What?

OLLIE   / But that's not.

            It's not.

            OLLIE *goes to kiss* ASHLEY. *She stops him.*

ASHLEY   Er, what are you doing?

OLLIE   Sorry. I thought.

I mean –

Now we've –

All of this has like, kind of all been a bit of a, you know.

A misunderstanding.

And that.

So –

ASHLEY   You thought we could just go back to the way it was before?

OLLIE   I dunno. Yeah, I spose.

I mean, why else did you…

The leaflet and that.

You must've known I'd…

ASHLEY   That's not what…

No.

No.

I did that for me.

OLLIE   What d'you mean?

ASHLEY   I…

I don't want to have to lie any more.

To pretend.

Cos it's…

It's exhausting.

Pretending everything's okay.

That you're something you're not.

It's exhausting.

Beat.

OLLIE	Yeah.

OLLIE   Yeah.

Yeah. I guess it is.

…

I wish you'd told me before.

ASHLEY   Cos you've got no secrets, have you?

OLLIE   Like what?

Have you been talking to Becky Forrester?

ASHLEY   What?

No.

OLLIE   Oh, right.

Cool.

ASHLEY   Your leg.

OLLIE   What about my leg?

ASHLEY   I don't know, what about it?

You were the one who thought I didn't want to have sex with you cos of it.

Beat. OLLIE *is uncomfortable.*

So?

OLLIE   …

ASHLEY   Ollie.

OLLIE   Yeah. Well. Nah.

I mean…

I thought maybe –

The way it looks.

Had put you off.

Cos it's…

You know.

Beat. OLLIE *and* ASHLEY *look at each other.*

ASHLEY   Take your trousers off.

OLLIE   What?

ASHLEY   Take them off.

OLLIE   Your parents are…

ASHLEY   Not like…

           Your leg.

           I want to see it.

OLLIE   No. No way.

ASHLEY   I've just like, turned myself inside out for you –

OLLIE   No! This is different.

           This is like, you know.

           No.

ASHLEY   Real?

OLLIE   That's not what I…

           No.

           I just…

ASHLEY   Fine.

           You should probably go then.

           An awkward OLLIE *reluctantly undoes his jeans
           and pulls them off. Pants on of course. He stands.
           Embarrassed by his body.* ASHLEY *studies him.*

           Ollie.

           You do know…

           There's nothing wrong with your leg.

OLLIE   If you…

           If you know what you're looking for.

           You can…

           See.

           Beat.

ASHLEY   No.

          You really can't.

OLLIE   Really?

ASHLEY   Nothing.

OLLIE   Right.

          Well.

          I feel like a massive twat now don't I?

          This is so embarrassing.

ASHLEY   D'you know what's really embarrassing?

          Being called a prick-tease.

          Being dumped on social media.

          Being stared at in the street after having 'slag'
          shouted at you.

          That's embarrassing.

          Silence. OLLIE *is ashamed.*

OLLIE   Yeah.

          I spose…

          I mean –

          Fuck.

          That was…

          I'm sorry.

          I am.

          That was…

          All of it.

          Out of order.

          Totally.

          I deserve to…

          Feel like a, a twat.

          Beat.

ASHLEY   Dad!

OLLIE   Oh my God!

           OLLIE *is horrified and hurriedly and sheepishly
           pulls his trousers up.* ASHLEY *laughs.*

ASHLEY   They've gone out.

           Didn't you hear the door?

OLLIE   That's not funny!

ASHLEY   Yes.

           It is.

OLLIE   Does that mean –

ASHLEY   Don't get any ideas.

           A moment. OLLIE *is deeply disappointed but
           knows how much he fucked up.*

           *He's still got the OCD leaflet in his hand. He
           offers it to* ASHLEY.

OLLIE   I spose you –

           D'you need this back?

           Beat.

ASHLEY   It could happen, but it'll be alright.

OLLIE   What?

ASHLEY   …

           It could happen, but it'll be alright.

           ASHLEY *looks at* OLLIE, *thinking. She takes the
           leaflet from him and rips it in half.*

OLLIE   Ash! Don't do that!

           Shouldn't you…

           Shouldn't you be like doing this with a doctor
           or…

ASHLEY   It'll be alright.

It could happen, but it'll be alright.

It could happen, but it'll be alright.

I'll be alright.

ASHLEY *tears the leaflet into tiny little pieces as hundreds of other leaflets flutter from the ceiling and onto the pair of them.*

Lights down.

A Nick Hern Book

Germ Free Adolescent first published as a paperback original in Great Britain in 2019 by Nick Hern Books Limited, The Glasshouse, 49a Goldhawk Road, London W12 8QP, in association with The Bunker Theatre

Germ Free Adolescent copyright © 2019 Natalie Mitchell

Natalie Mitchell has asserted her right to be identified as the author of this work

Cover design by David Ralf

Designed and typeset by Nick Hern Books, London
Printed in the UK by Mimeo Ltd, Huntingdon, Cambridgeshire PE29 6XX

A CIP catalogue record for this book is available from the British Library

ISBN 978 1 84842 913 0

www.nickhernbooks.co.uk

facebook.com/nickhernbooks

twitter.com/nickhernbooks